Cool Restaurants London

teNeues

Imprint

Many thanks to Simon Willis (Great Eastern Hotel), Samir Kadi (Metropolitan Hotel), Guy Dittrich and all other London insiders for their recommendations and assistance. Special thanks to all restaurant owners, chefs, architects and designers for their generous support.

Editor: Martin Nicholas Kunz
Editorial coordination: Patricia Massó

Photos (location): Ian Schrager Hotels (Asia de Cuba food, Spoon at Sanderson page 116 & food), Richard Leeney (Atlantic Bar and Grill), Network London (Aurora, EightOverEight food), Anouska Hempel Design (Blakes food), Softroom (Café Consort), Fritz von der Schulenburg (Chintamani), Jean Cazals (Cinnamon Club food), courtesy E&O (food), courtesy Eat and two veg, David Loftus (Fifteen food, Isola page 74, 75), Graham Jepson (Fifth Floor food), James McCauley (Isola page 76, 77), Jason Lowe (Locanda Locatelli food), Geraldine Dean-Dorat (Momo Special), courtesy Nobu (food), Sauce Communications (Shumi), courtesy Sketch, courtesy Tom Aikens (food), courtesy Ubon (page 125 & food), courtesy Zuma. All other Photos by Roland Bauer and Martin Nicholas Kunz.

Introduction: Guy Dittrich

Layout & Pre-press: Thomas Hausberg
Imaging: Florian Höch, Jan Hausberg

Translations: Ade Team, Margarita Celdràn-Kuhl (Spanish, German), Dominique Santoro (French)

Published by teNeues Publishing Group

teNeues Publishing Company
16 West 22nd Street, New York, NY 10010, USA
Tel.: 001-212-627-9090, Fax: 001-212-627-9511

teNeues Book Division
Kaistraße 18
40221 Düsseldorf, Germany
Tel.: 0049-(0)211-994597-0, Fax: 0049-(0)211-994597-40

teNeues Publishing UK Ltd.
P.O. Box 402
West Byfleet
KT14 7ZF, Great Britain
Tel.: 0044-1932-403509, Fax: 0044-1932-403514

www.teneues.com

ISBN: 3-8238-4568-3

© 2003 teNeues Verlag GmbH + Co. KG, Kempen

Printed in Italy

Bibliographic information published by Die Deutsche Bibliothek. Die Deutsche Bibliothek lists this publication in the Deutsche Nationalbibliografie; detailed bibliographic data is available in the Internet at http://dnb.ddb.de.

Content	Page

Introduction

Few places in the world can match the eclecticism of London's restaurant scene. Burgeoning affluence and greater traveling experiences have generated demand for new and different cuisines that restaurateurs have seized upon. Guests are able to choose Asian-Latino, South American or Italian influenced Japanese, British with an Italian Mediterranean slant, modern Indian, French, Chinese or Moroccan, or even just make up their own dishes. There's no escaping the fact that the food, its quality, presentation and service are still the key to the ultimate success of a restaurant but these factors are now essentials. Diners are looking beyond these accepted prerequisites when making their choices.

It is the place, the restaurant that is increasingly important. What differentiates the restaurants listed in this edition of *Cool Restaurants London* is their interior design and architectural make up.

Just as the cuisines vary so too do the designs. Take the muted elegance of David Collins' hemispherical, cream leather banquets and concave mirrors at Locanda Locatelli, the dark and moody atmosphere that is Christian Liaigre's mark at Hakkasan, the grandeur of the high ceilings and columns at Sir Terence Conran's Aurora or the Atlantic Bar & Grill, the restored parquet flooring at the Cinnamon Club or that of the ceilings of Isola, the use of the river view at Ubon or, further upstream, at Putney Bridge, or the granite boulders, buttressing the sushi counters at Noriyoshi Muramatsu's Zuma. Locations have been as wide-ranging for the architects—from pride of place in some of London's finest hotels to a place on the high street for others. There's a lot more to it than just eating!

So, relax and enjoy this insight into the world of food and design—take in the complete experience.

Guy Dittrich

Einleitung

Es gibt nur wenige Orte auf der Welt, die mit dem Eklektizismus der Londoner Restaurantszene mithalten können. Aufkommender Wohlstand und ausgedehnte Reisen schufen eine Nachfrage nach neuen, andersartigen Kochkünsten, die von den Gastronomen aufgegriffen wurde. Die Gäste haben die Wahl zwischen asiatisch-lateinamerikanischer Küche, japanischer Küche mit südamerikanischen oder italienischen Einflüssen, britischer Kochkunst mit mediterranem Einschlag und moderner indischer, französischer, chinesischer oder marokkanischer Küche – oder sie können sogar ihre eigenen Gerichte zusammenstellen. Es ist eine unumstößliche Tatsache, dass die Speisen, ihre Qualität, Präsentation und der Service letztendlich der Schlüssel zum Erfolg eines Restaurants darstellen, jedoch nur als grundlegende Faktoren anzusehen sind. Die Gäste lassen sich bei ihrer Wahl von weit mehr als diesen allgemein anerkannten Grundvoraussetzungen leiten.

Eine immer bedeutendere Rolle spielt der Ort, das Restaurant. Die in dieser Ausgabe von *Cool Restaurants London* vorgestellten Restaurants unterscheiden sich durch ihre Inneneinrichtung und Architektur.

Wie bei der Küche, gibt es auch bei der Einrichtung eine große Vielfalt. Die schlichte Eleganz von David Collins' halbkugelförmigen, in cremeweißem Leder gehaltenen Speisesälen mit den konkaven Spiegeln im Locanda Locatelli, die dunkel-düstere Atmosphäre, die Christian Liaigres Hakkasan kennzeichnet, die erhabene Pracht der hohen Decken und Säulen in Sir Terence Conrans Aurora oder Atlantic Bar & Grill, die restaurierten Parkettböden im Cinnamon Club oder die Decken im Isola, der Flussblick im Ubon oder – weiter stromaufwärts – im Putney Bridge, oder die Granitblöcke, die als Stützpfeiler für die Sushi-Theken in Noriyoshi Muramatsus Zuma dienen. Auch bei der Standortwahl zeigen die Architekten eine große Vielfalt – vom erstklassigen Platz in einigen von Londons besten Hotels bis hin zum Restaurant an der Hauptstraße. Es braucht mehr als nur das bloße Speisen!

Entspannen Sie sich und genießen Sie die Einblicke in die Welt der Kochkunst und des Designs – lassen Sie diese Einheit auf sich wirken.

Guy Dittrich

Introduction

Peu de métropoles dans le monde atteignent, en matière de restaurants, l'é-clectisme de la scène londonienne. Une affluence assurée et une plus grande expérience des voyages ont engendré une demande en faveur de cuisines nouvelles et différentes, demande que les restaurateurs se sont empressés de satisfaire. Les convives ont le choix entre des cuisines asiatico-latines, de la cuisine japonaise sous influence sud-africaine ou italienne, de la cuisine britannique avec une tendance italianisante et méditerranéenne, et des cuisines modernes indienne, française, chinoise ou marocaine, ou préparer simple-ment eux-mêmes leurs plats. Que les denrées, leur qualité, leur présentation et le service demeurent la clé du succès d'un restaurant en définitive, de-meure un fait incontournable ; il s'agit de caractéristiques essentielles, mais pas plus. Lorsque les convives font leur choix, ils regardent au-delà de ces conditions préalables par ailleurs acceptées.

C'est le site, le restaurant lui-même qui acquiert une importance croissante. Ce qui distingue les restaurants énumérés dans cette édition de *Cool Restau-rants London*, c'est l'esthétisme de leurs intérieurs et l'architecture de leurs aménagements.

Les designs changent comme les cuisines. Prenez l'élégance discrète des banquettes hémisphériques en cuir crème chez David Collins, les miroirs con-caves de Locanda Locatelli, l'atmosphère tamisée mais très à la mode, vérita-ble griffe de Christian Liaigre à l'Hakkasan, la grandeur des plafonds et colon-nes hautes à l'Aurora de Sir Terence Conran, ou encore l'Atlantic Bar & Grill, les parquets restaurés du Cinnamon Club ou le revêtement des plafonds d'Isola, la mise en valeur de la vue sur la Tamise à l'Ubon ou, en remontant la rivière, à Putney Bridge, ou les rochers de granit flanquant les comptoirs à sushi du Zuma de Noriyoshi Muramatsu. Les sites couvrent aussi une gamme architecturale très large. Certains, prestigieux, hébergent les plus grands hô-tels de Londres, d'autres se situent sur la rue principale. Tous ont infiniment plus à offrir que la dégustation de plats.

Détendez-vous, donc, et profitez de cette visite guidée dans le monde de la gastronomie et du design, faites-en l'expérience intégrale.

Guy Dittrich

Introducción

Pocos lugares en el mundo alcanzan el nivel de eclecticismo del panorama de los restaurantes londinenses. La floreciente prosperidad y el incremento de las experiencias de viaje han generado una demanda de cocinas nuevas y diferentes a la que los restauradores han sabido responder. Los comensales pueden elegir entre los estilos asiático-latino, sudamericano o japonés con influencias italianas, británico con un toque italiano del mediterráneo, indio moderno, francés, chino o marroquí, o incluso llegar a componer sus propios platos. A nadie se le escapa ya que la comida, su calidad, presentación y servicio siguen siendo la clave para el éxito definitivo de un restaurante, pero ahora esos factores se han convertido en un elemento esencial. Los clientes buscan algo aparte de estos prerrequisitos generalmente aceptados a la hora de hacer su elección.

Un elemento cada vez más importante es el propio lugar físico, el restaurante en sí. Lo que diferencia a los restaurantes que aparecen en esta edición de *Cool Restaurants London* es su diseño de interiores y su esquema arquitectónico.

Los diseños son tan variados como las cocinas. Se puede optar por la serena elegancia de las banquetas semiesféricas de cuero color crema y los espejos cóncavos de David Collins en Locanda Locatelli, el ambiente oscuro y taciturno que confiere el sello distintivo de Christian Liaigre al Hakkasan, la grandiosidad de los altos techos y las columnas del Aurora o el Atlantic Bar & Grill de Sir Terence Conran, el renovado revestimiento de parqué empleado en el Cinnamon Club o los techos de Isola, el uso de las vistas al río que se hace en Ubon o, más arriba, en Putney Bridge, o las piezas de granito que sustentan los mostradores de sushi en el Zuma, de Noriyoshi Muramatsu. Las ubicaciones varían también tanto como los arquitectos, pasando desde el orgullo de poder estar en uno de los mejores hoteles de Londres para algunos, hasta poder hacerse con un hueco en las principales calles para otros. ¡Y es que la comida no lo es todo!

Así que reléjense y disfruten de esta oportunidad de conocer el mundo de la restauración y el diseño en una misma experiencia completa.

Guy Dittrich

Asia de Cuba

Design: Philippe Starck I Chef: Owen Stewart

45 St Martins Lane I Covent Garden, WC2N 4HX
Phone: +44 20 7300 5588
www.asiadecuba-restaurant.com
Tube: Leicester Square
Opening hours: Lunch Mon–Fri 12 noon to 2:30 pm, dinner Mon–Sat 5:30 pm to
12 midnight, dinner Sun 5:30 pm to 10:30 pm
Average price: £55
Cuisine: Asian, Cuban

Wok Crispy Fish

Knuspriger Fisch aus dem Wok
Wok poisson friteuse
Wok pescado fríe

1 striped bass, butchered 1½ lb
3 oz flour mix
3 oz marinade
3 oz 60/40 crabmeat blend
¼ cup roasted red pepper sauce
tsp black sesame seeds
tsp chives
1 banana leaf cut into diamond
¼ oz scallions, julienned
3 cups/1 cup ratio flour to cornstarch with salt and pepper

Dredge a 1½ lb sea bass in 3 oz of flour/cornstarch mixture. Remove excess flour and place into the 200 °C (400 °F) fryer. Cook until golden brown and crisp. Remove from fryer and drain on a paper towel or cloth. Hold warm. While fish is in the fryer, heat up 3 oz of marinade with ¼ cup of red pepper sauce. Add 3 oz of the crab meat and warm through. Hold warm. On a rectangle plate, place a long rectangle banana leaf on the bottom and ladle ¼ cup of red pepper sauce on top. Garnish the sauce with a tsp of black sesame seeds. Place the fish standing on its belly in the center of the plate. Make sure the fish is stable by adjusting the bottom where it is gutted. Spoon the hot marinade into the top cavity of the fish. Garnish with the tsp of chopped chives. Place a ¼ oz of julienne scallions by the head of the fish.

1 Wolfsbarsch, ausgenommen 680 g
85 g Mehlmischung
85 g Marinade
85 g 60/40 Krabbenfleischmischung
¼ Tasse geröstete rote Paprikasoße
TL schwarzer Sesam
TL Schnittlauch
1 Bananenblatt, gewürfelt
7 g Frühlingszwiebeln, in Julienne geschnitten
3 Tassen/1 Tasse 3:1 Verhältnis Mehl zu Speisestärke mit Salz und Pfeffer

Einen 680 g schweren Wolfsbarsch in einer 85 g Mischung aus Mehl und Speisestärke wenden. Das überschüssige Mehl entfernen und den Wolfsbarsch in die 200 °C heiße Bratpfanne geben. Solange braten bis er goldbraun und knusprig ist. Aus der Pfanne nehmen und auf einem Papier- oder Küchentuch abtropfen lassen. Warm halten. Während der Fisch in der Pfanne ist, 85 g Marinade mit einer ¼ Tasse der roten Paprikasoße erwärmen. 85 g Krabbenfleisch hinzugeben und alles warm halten. Ein langes Bananenblatt auf einen rechteckigen Teller legen und ¼ Tasse der roten Paprikasoße auf dem Blatt verteilen. Die Soße mit einem TL schwarzen Sesams verzieren. Den Fisch, mit dem Bauch nach unten, in die Mitte des Tellers legen. Platzieren Sie dabei die ausgenommene Unterseite so, dass der Fisch nicht umkippen kann. Gießen Sie anschließend die heiße Marinade in die obere Öffnung des Fisches. Garnieren Sie nun mit einem Teelöffel den geschnittenen Schnittlauch und bringen Sie am Kopf des Fisches die in Julienne geschnittenen Frühlingszwiebeln an.

1 Bar d'Amérique, apprêté par le poisson-
nier, 680 g
85 g mélange de farine
85 g marinade
85 g mélange de chair de crabe 60/40
¼ de tasse sauce au piment rouge grillé
c. à café graines de sésame noir
c. à café ciboulette
1 feuille de bananier coupée en rhombes
7 g julienne d'oignons verts
3 tasses/1 tasse 3 tasses de farine,
1 tasse d'amidon de maïs
salez et poivrez

Saupoudrez 85 g du mélange de farine et
d'amidon de maïs sur un bar commun de
680 g. Retirez la farine excédentaire et
déposez-le dans la friteuse à 200 °C.
Faites cuire jusqu'à ce que la surface
enfarinée soit bien dorée et croustillante.
Retirez le poisson de la friteuse. Faites
chauffer 85 g de marinade avec ¼ de
tasse de sauce au piment rouge grillé.
Ajoutez 85 g de la chair de crabe et faites
chauffer à cœur. Maintenez au chaud. Sur
un plat rectangulaire, placez une feuille de
bananier longue puis, à la louche, versez
l'équivalent d'un quart de tasse de la
sauce au piment rouge grillé. Garnissez
cette sauce avec une cuiller à café de
graines de sésame noir. Disposez le poisson au centre du plat, en appui sur le ventre. Assurez-vous que le poisson se main-
tienne de façon stable : ajustez la partie
du ventre éviscérée. A la cuiller, versez la
marinade chaud dans la cavité supérieure
du poisson. Garnissez avec une cuiller à
café de ciboulette hachée. Placez 7 g de
la julienne d'oignons verts près de la tête
du poisson.

1 lubina cortada en tiras de 680 g
85 g de mezcla de harinas
85 g de escabeche
85 g de 60/40 de carne de cangrejo
¼ taza de salsa de pimienta de cayena
tostada
1 cucharadita de semillas de sésamo
negro
1 cucharadita de cebollinos
1 hoja de plátano cortada en rombos
7 g de chalotes en juliana
3 tazas/1 taza mezcla al 3:1 de harina y
maicena salpimentada

Rebozar una lubina de 680 g con 85 g de
la mezcla de harina y maicena. Eliminar el
exceso de harina e introducirla en la freidora a 200 °C. Cocinar hasta que esté
dorada y crujiente. Sacar de la freidora y
dejar secar sobre un papel de cocina o un
trapo. Mantener caliente. Mientras el pescado se fríe, calentar 85 g de escabeche
con ¼ de taza de salsa de pimientos.
Añadir 85 g de carne de cangrejo y calentar. Mantener caliente. En una fuente rec-
tangular, colocar un rectángulo largo de
hoja de plátano sobre el fondo y verter ¼
de taza de salsa de pimientos encima.
Guarnecer la salsa con una cucharadita de
semillas de sésamo negro. Colocar el pescado boca abajo en el centro de la fuente.
Asegurarse de que el pescado está en una
posición estable ajustando la parte inferior
donde se ha vaciado para limpiarlo. Verter
el escabeche caliente en la cavidad supe-
rior del pescado. Guarnecer con la cucharadita de cebollinos picados. Colocar
aprox. 7 g de chalotes en juliana junto a la
cabeza del pescado.

Atlantic Bar and Grill

Design: Origin by Oliver Bernard 1934,
refurnished by Shaun Clarkson 2003 | Owner: Oliver Peyton
Chef: Ben O'Donoghue

20 Glasshouse Street | Soho, W1R 5RQ
Phone: +44 20 7734 4888
Tube: Piccadilly Circus
Opening hours: Lunch Mon–Fri 12 noon to 3 pm, Dinner Mon–Sat 6 pm to
11:30 pm, not open on Sunday | Bar: 12 noon to 3 am
Average price: £44
Cuisine: Modern British

Aurora

Design: Conran & Partners | Chef: Warren Geraghty

40 Liverpool Street | City-North, EC2M 7QN
Phone: +44 20 7618 7000
www.aurora-restaurant.co.uk | restaurantres@great-eastern-hotel.co.uk
Tube: Liverpool Street
Opening hours: Mon–Fri 12 noon to 2:45 pm & 6:45 pm to 10 pm
Average price: £38
Cuisine: Modern European

Ballotine

of foie gras, celeriac & aubergine

Ballotine aus Gänseleber, Knollensellerie und Aubergine
Ballotine de foie gras, de céleri-rave et d'aubergine
Ballotine de foie gras, apio nabo y berenjena

1 lb 1½ oz lobe Ardignac foie gras	500 g Lappen Ardignac-Gänseleber
1 celeriac	1 Knollensellerie
1 aubergine	1 Aubergine
5 oz Mesclun salad	150 g Mesclun Salat
3½ oz dried wild mushrooms	100 g wilde Champignons, getrocknet
100 ml balsamic vinegar	100 ml Balsamico
50 ml sweet wine	50 ml süßer Wein
25 ml white port	25 ml weißer Portwein
25 ml brandy	25 ml Brandy
salt/sugar	Salz/Zucker
Chinese five spice	chinesische Gewürzmischung
Mayonnaise	Majonnaise

Leave the lobe of foie gras out to reach room temperature. Once it is soft with a thin handle of a spoon remove all the veins and arteries whilst trying to keep the lobe as whole as possible. Season the lobe with salt, sugar and little fine sprinkle of Chinese five spice, then add the sweet wine, brandy and port. Cover tightly with cling film and marinate in the fridge for 24 hours. Slice the aubergine in half, score across the flesh, add thin slices of garlic into the incisions, sprinkle thyme, salt, pepper and olive oil. Wrap in tinfoil and bake in a low oven for 1 hour. Remove the flesh from the skin and mix with an equal quantity of mayonnaise. Slice the celeriac as thin as possible on a mandoline then cut into discs. Place in a pan and cover with balsamic vinegar and reduce down to syrup. Remove from the stove and leave to cool. Add a few drops of truffle oil and just cover with peanut oil, season and leave to cool. Plac the foie gras on a tray and put into a cool oven 150 °C (365 °F) for 10–12 minutes to render the fat, remove from the oven and strain off the butter. Roll into sausages (approx 2 inches in diameter) and place into iced water to set. When set remove from cling film, roll in powder and wrap again.

Die Gänseleber aus dem Kühlschrank nehmen und warten, bis sie Zimmertemperatur erreicht hat. Nachdem sie weich geworden ist, die Venen und Arterien mit einem Löffelgriff entfernen und darauf achten, dass die Form der Leber möglichst erhalten bleibt. Die Leber mit Salz, Zucker und einer feinen Prise chinesischer Gewürzmischung bestreuen. Anschließend den süßen Wein, den Brandy und den Portwein hinzufügen. Mit einer Frischhaltefolie abdecken und 24 Stunden im Kühlschrank marinieren lassen. Die Aubergine halbieren und das Fleisch einschneiden. Dünne Knoblauchscheiben in die Zwischenräume geben und mit Thymian, Salz, Pfeffer und Olivenöl würzen. In Alufolie einwickeln und 1 Stunde bei schwacher Hitze backen. Die Haut ablösen und das Fleisch mit der gleichen Menge Majonnaise vermischen. Hobeln Sie den Knollensellerie mit der Mandoline so dünn es geht und schneiden Sie ihn anschließend in runde Scheiben. Den Knollensellerie in eine Pfanne geben, mit Balsamicoessig bedecken und so lange köcheln lassen, bis er sämig wird. Die Pfanne von der Herdplatte nehmen und abkühlen lassen. Ein paar Tropfen Trüffelöl beigeben, mit Erdnussöl bedecken und würzen. Abkühlen lassen. Die Gänseleber in eine Auflaufform geben und in den mittelwarmen Ofen (150 °C) 10–12 Minuten backen, um das Fett auszulassen. Aus dem Ofen nehmen und das Fett abschöpfen. Aus der Leber Röllchen formen (ca. 5 cm Ø) und in eiskaltes Wasser legen, damit die Form erhalten bleibt. Frischhaltefolie entfernen, die Röllchen mit der Gewürzmischung bestäuben und wieder einwickeln.

Lobe de foie gras Ardignac de 500 g
1 céleri-rave
1 aubergine
150 g de mesclun de salade
100 g de champignons sauvages secs
100 ml de vinaigre balsamique
50 ml de vin doux
25 ml de porto blanc
25 ml d'eau-de-vie de raisin
Sel/sucre
Cinq épices chinoises
Mayonnaise

Laissez le lobe de foie gras hors du réfrigé-rateur pour qu'il prenne la température de la pièce. Une fois qu'il est mou, retirez-en toutes les veines et artères à l'aide d'un manche de cuillère fin, tout en veillant à ce que le lobe conserve si possible son inté-grité. Assaisonnez-le avec le sel, le sucre et saupoudrez-le un peu et finement des cinq épices chinoises, ajoutez ensuite le vin doux, l'eau-de-vie et le porto. Couvrez hermétiquement avec un ruban adhésif et faites mariner au réfrigérateur pendant 24 heures. Partagez les aubergines en deux, incisez leur chair et insérez dedans de fines tranches d'ail, parsemez de thym, de sel, de poivre et d'huile d'olive. Enveloppez les aubergines dans une feuille d'aluminium et faites-les cuire pendant une heure. Détachez leur peau puis passez leur chair au mixer à laquelle vous aurez ajouté une quantité égale de mayonnaise. Coupez le céleri-rave en très fines tranches à l'aide d'un disque à émincer, puis découpez-les en rondelles. Placez-les dans une poêle où vous aurez versé le vinaigre balsamique et réduisez jusqu'à obtenir un sirop. Retirez la poêle du feu et laissez-la refroidir. Ajoutez un peu d'huile aux truffes et recouvrez à peine d'huile d'arachide, assaisonnez et laissez refroidir. Déposez le foie gras sur une plaque et placez-le dans un four moyen-nement chaud (150 °C) pendant 10 à 12 minutes pour qu'il dégraisse, retirez-le ensuite du four puis filtrez le gras. Roulez le foie en saucisses (d'env. 2 pouces de diamètre) puis déposez-les dans de l'eau glacée pour qu'elles s'affermissent. Une fois affermies, retirez la pellicule adhéren-te, roulez-les dans la poudre et enveloppez-les à nouveau.

500 g de foie gras Ardignac en un lóbulo
1 apio nabo
1 berenjena
150 g de ensalada Mesclun
100 g de champiñones silvestres secos
100 ml de vinagre balsámico
50 ml de vino dulce
25 ml de oporto blanco
25 ml de brandy
Sal/azúcar
Cinco especias chinas
Mayonesa

Dejar el foie gras a temperatura ambiente. Una vez que esté blando eliminar todas las venas y arterias con un instrumento fino tratando de mantener en la medida de lo posible la forma del lóbulo. Aderezar el foie gras con sal, azúcar y un poco de las cinco especias chinas. Luego, agregar el vino dulce, el brandy y el oporto. Cubrir con film transparente y dejar macerar en el frigorífico durante 24 horas. Trocear la berenjena en rodajas por la mitad, hacer unos cortes en la carne e introducir unas rodajitas finas de ajo dentro de las incisio-nes, aderezar con tomillo, sal, pimienta y aceite de oliva. Envolver con papel de estaño y cocinar en el horno a fuego bajo durante 1 hora. Separar la carne de la piel y mezclar con una cantidad igual de mayo-nesa. Cortar el apio nabo en rodajas lo más finas posibles usando una mandolina, y luego cortar en discos. Colocar en una sartén y cubrir con vinagre balsámico, dejando que se reduzca a un líquido espe-so. Retirar y dejar enfriar. Añadir unas gotas de aceite de trufa y cubrir con acei-te de cacahuete, aderezar y dejar enfriar. Colocar el foie gras sobre una bandeja e introducir en el horno no muy caliente (150 °C) durante 10–12 minutos para de-rretir la grasa. Luego, sacarlo del horno y filtrar la manteca. Enrollar en forma de sal-chichas (de aprox. 5 centímetros de diá-metro) y colocar bajo agua helada para que mantengan la forma. Cuando estén bien formadas, sacar del papel de estaño, espolvorear y volver a envolver.

Blakes Restaurant

Design: Anouska Hempel | Chef: Neville Campbell

33 Roland Gardens | South Kensington, SW7 3PF
Phone: +44 20 7370 6701
www.blakeshotels.com
Tube: Gloucester Road or South Kensington
Opening hours: Mon–Sun 12:30 pm to 5:30 pm & 7:30 pm to 10:45 pm
Average price: £53
Cuisine: French Fired Fusion

Blakes

Classic Bento Box

Blakes klassische Bento Box
Blakes Classic Bento Box
Bento Box clásico de Blakes

Ginger broth:
1 bunch coriander stalks
10 sticks lemon grass
10–15 red chilies
2 pieces of ginger
2 pieces of galangal
5 shallots
3 tomatoes
10 Kaffir lime leaves
5 prawn shells
12 l chicken stock
Fish sauce
Sugar
Lime juice
Garnish—pickled ginger, ginger crisp, lime twist

Put all the ingredients for the hot and sour stock into a pot and bring to the boil. Reduce the heat and reduce slowly down to 3 litres of stock. Season with fish sauce, sugar and lime juice. To serve, boil hot and sour stock with pickled ginger. Blitz and pass through a fine chinois. Bring back to the boil. Garnish with a white Udon Noodle, ginger crisp, pickled ginger and a lime twist. Peking Duck pancake wraps: Blanche rice paper and refresh, slice a pink cooked duck breast, Hoisin sauce, cucumber batons, julienne of spring onions, chives, coriander. Salmon Sashimi with a blood orange and ginger vinaigrette: Thinly slice 4 pieces of salmon and square off. Garnish with a few sprigs of coriander, lamb's lettuce and julienne of spring onions. Serve with a side dip of ginger and blood orange vinaigrette. Green rice: Garnish—Deep fried mint. Serve with a side dip of Hoisin sauce.

Ingwerbrühe:
1 Bund Korianderstängel
10 Zweige Zitronengras
10–15 rote Chilischoten
2 Stück Ingwer
2 Stück Galangal
5 Schalotten
3 Tomaten
10 Kaffir Limonenblätter
5 Garnelenschalen
12 l Hühnerbrühe
Fischsoße
Zucker
Limettensaft
Garnierung – Ingwer, in Essig eingelegt, Ingwer-Chips, Limettenscheiben in Spiralform

Alle Zutaten für die scharfe, saure Brühe in einen Topf geben und zum Kochen bringen. Die Hitze reduzieren und die Brühe bis auf 3 Liter runterkochen lassen. Mit Fischsoße, Zucker und Limettensaft würzen. Zum Servieren, die scharfe, saure Brühe mit in Essig eingelegtem Ingwer kochen. Danach durch ein Spitzsieb passieren und erneut zum Kochen bringen. Garnieren Sie mit weißen Udon-Nudeln, Ingwer Chips, in Essig eingelegtem Ingwer und spiralförmig geschnittenen Limettenscheiben. Peking Ente-Crêpes: Reispapier blanchieren und abschrecken, eine rosa gebratene Entenbrust in Scheiben schneiden, Hoisin Sauce, Gurkenstreifen, Frühlingszwiebeln, in Julienne-Streifen geschnitten, Schnittlauch und Koriander hinzufügen. Sashimi Lachs mit einer Blutorange und Ingwer Vinaigrette: Den Lachs in 4 dünne Scheiben schneiden und würfeln. Garnieren Sie mit ein paar Korianderzweigen, Feldsalat und in Julienne geschnittenen Frühlingszwiebeln. Servieren Sie mit einem Dip aus Ingwer und Blutorangen. Grüner Reis: Garnierung – gebratene Minze mit einem Dip aus Hoisin Sauce servieren.

Bouillon de gingembre :
1 bouquet de pédoncules de coriandre
10 tiges de citronnelle
10–15 chillis rouges
2 morceaux de gingembre
2 morceaux de Galangal
5 échalotes
3 tomates
10 feuilles de kafir lime
5 crevettes étêtées
12 l de bouillon de poulet
Sauce de poisson
Sucre
Jus de lime douce
Garniture : marinade de gingembre, croustilles de gingembre, torsade de lime

Mettez tous les ingrédients du bouillon
pimenté et aigre dans une casserole à
bords hauts et faites bouillir. Baissez le feu
et faites réduire lentement jusqu'à ce qu'il
ne reste plus que 3 litres de bouillon.
Assaisonnez-le avec la sauce de poisson, le
sucre et le jus de lime douce. Pour servir,
faites bouillir le bouillon pimenté et aigre
avec le gingembre mariné. Passez ensuite
au chinois fin. Remettez à bouillir.
Garnissez avec des pâtes Udon fines, les
croustilles de gingembre, le gingembre
mariné et une torsade de lime. Crêpes rou-
lées pour canard de Pékin : Blanchir le papier de riz et le rafraîchir, couper en tranches du blanc de canard cuit rosé, Sauce
Hoisin, bâtonnets de concombre, julienne
d'oignons printaniers, ciboulette, coriandre.
Sashimi de saumon avec un orange sanguine et de la vinaigrette au gingembre :
Coupez 4 tranches fines de saumon et for-
mez des carrés. Garnissez avec quelques
tiges de coriandre, de mâche et avec des
oignons printaniers découpés en julienne.
Servez sur le côté une trempette faite de
vinaigrette aux gingembres et à l'orange
sanguine. Riz vert : Garniture – Menthe
surgelée. Servez avec une trempette faite
de sauce Hoisin et placée sur le côté.

Caldo de jengibre:
1 ramillete de tallos de cilantro
10 palos de limoncillo
10–15 chiles rojos
2 trozos de jengibre
2 trozos de galangal
5 chalotas
3 tomates
10 hojas de lima kaffir
5 cáscaras de langostino
12 l de caldo de pollo
Salsa de pescado
Azúcar
Zumo de lima
Guarnición: jengibre en conserva, crujiente
de jengibre, una rodajita de lima

Colocar todos los ingredientes del caldo
agrio y caliente en una olla y llevar a ebullición. Bajar la temperatura y reducir len-
tamente a 3 litros de caldo. Aderezar con
la salsa de pescado, el azúcar y el zumo
de lima. Para servir, cocer el caldo con el
jengibre en conserva. Pasar a través de un
chino fino. Volver a llevar a ebullición.
Aderezar con fideos chinos blancos udon,
el crujiente de jengibre, el jengibre en conserva y una rodajita de lima. Rollitos de
pato Pekín: Escaldar el papel de arroz y
refrescar, cortar en rodajas una pechuga
de pato ligeramente cocinada, salsa
Hoisin, bastones de pepino, juliana de
cebolletas, cebollinos, cilantro. Salmón
Sashimi con vinagreta de naranja de sangre y jengibre: Cortar en rodajas finas 4
trozos de salmón y darles forma de cuadra-
do. Guarnecer con unos tallos de cilantro,
canónigos y la juliana de cebolletas. Servir
con la vinagreta de naranja de sangre y
jengibre a un lado. Arroz verde: Guarnición
–Menta frita. Servir con salsa Hoisin a un
lado.

Café Consort

Design: Softroom | Chef: Andrew Norris

Royal Albert Hall, Kensington Gore | Kensington SW7 2AP
Phone: +44 207 589 8212
www.royalalberthall.com
Tube: South Kensington
Opening hours: 2 hours before shows
Cuisine: Contemporary

Chintamani

Design: Zeynep Fadillioglu | Chef: David Jones

122 Jermyn Street | St James's, SW1Y 4UJ
Phone: +44 20 7839 2020
Tube: Piccadilly Circus
Opening hours: Mon–Sat 12 noon to 3:30 pm & 6 pm to 1 am
Price range: Starters £4,50 – £11, main £14 – £22, dessert £7
Average price: £47
Cuisine: Middle Eastern

The Cinnamon Club

Design: David Gabriel | Chef: Vivek Singh

The Old Westminster Library, Great Smith Street | Westminster, SW1P 3BU
Phone: +44 20 7222 2555
www.cinnamonclub.com | info@cinnamonclub.com
Tube: Westminster, St James's Park
Opening hours: Mon–Fri breakfast 7:30 am to 10 am, lunch 12 noon to 3 pm,
dinner 6 pm to 11 pm, Sat dinner 6 pm to 11 pm, Sun 2 pm to 4 pm
Average price: £40
Cuisine: Indian

Grilled Half Lobster
Bengali style

Gegrillte Hummerhälfte Bengali
Demi-homard cuit à la mode Bengalie
Bogavante a la parrilla al estilo Bengalí

<table>
<tr><td>

2 lobsters, cut into half lengthways. Ask your fishmonger to do this for you. Crack the claw and keep the meat aside.
1 tsp veg or corn oil
1 tsp salt
1 tsp green cardamom powder
1 tsp sugar
Juice of one lemon
2/3 oz chopped fresh green coriander
1 tsp coconut milk

For the claw meat:
1 tsp oil
1 onion finely chopped
1 inch piece of finely chopped ginger
1 finely chopped medium sized tomato
1 tsp red chilli powder
1 tsp salt

</td><td>

2 Hummer, längs in zwei Hälften schneiden. Bitten Sie Ihren Fischverkäufer, dies für Sie zu übernehmen. Brechen Sie die Zange und nehmen Sie das Fleisch heraus.
1 TL pflanzliches Öl oder Maisöl
1 TL Salz
1 TL grünes Kardamompulver
1 TL Zucker
Limettensaft
20 g geschnittener frischer, grüner Koriander
1 TL Kokosnussmilch

Für das Zangenfleisch :
1 TL Öl
1 Zwiebel, fein geschnitten
1 Stück (2,5 cm) Ingwer, fein geschnitten
1 mittelgroße Tomate, fein geschnitten
1 TL rotes Chilipulver
1 TL Salz

</td></tr>
</table>

Clean and pat dry the lobsters and keep aside. Heat oil in a large frying pan, put the lobsters in the pan flesh side down and let it sear for a couple of minutes or until the meat sears well and just starts to take color. Take the lobsters out of the pan and sprinkle with salt, green cardamom powder, sugar, green coriander, and drizzle with coconut milk. Place the half lobster under the grill and serve when cooked (usually 8–10 minutes under the grill should be fine). For the claw, heat oil in a pan, add onions and sauté until golden brown, add the lobster claw and stir fry quickly on high heat. Add the ginger and sauté for a couple of minutes more, adding the tomatoes and cook until the mix is dry. Add salt, check consistency and serve in the lobster head.

Die Hummer reinigen, trocken tupfen und beiseite legen. Öl in eine große Bratpfanne geben, die Hummer mit dem Fleisch nach unten legen. Braten lassen, bis das Fleisch gar ist und anfängt, Farbe anzunehmen. Nehmen Sie nun die Hummer aus der Pfanne und würzen Sie mit Salz, grünem Kardamompulver, Zucker und grünem Koriander und beträufeln Sie den Hummer anschließend mit Kokosnussmilch. Schieben Sie die Hummerhälfte in den Grill. Servieren, sobald sie gar ist (normalerweise sollten 8–10 Minuten im Grill ausreichen). Für die Zange wird das Öl mit den Zwiebeln in der Pfanne erhitzt, bis sie goldbraun sind. Dann gibt man die Hummerzange hinzu, die bei starker Hitze kurz angebraten wird. Ingwer hinzufügen und noch ein paar Minuten rösten. Tomaten hineingeben und garen, bis der Saft aus der Mischung verkocht ist. Salzen Sie, prüfen Sie die Konsistenz und servieren Sie die Mischung im Kopf des Hummers.

2 homards partagés en deux dans le sens
de la longueur. Demandez à votre poisson-
nier d'effectuer cette opération. Brisez la
pince et mettez sa chair de côté.
1 c. à café d'huile végétale ou de maïs
1 c. à café de sel
1 c. à café de poudre de cardamome verte
1 c. à café de sucre
Le jus d'un citron
20 g de coriandre fraîchement haché
1 c. à café de lait de noix de coco

Pour la chair de la pince :
1 c. à café d'huile
1 oignon finement haché
1 morceau de gingembre (2,5 cm),
finement haché
1 tomate de taille moyenne finement
hachée
1 c. à café de poudre de chilli rouge
1 c. à café de sel

Nettoyez les homards et tamponnez-les pour
les sécher puis mettez-les de côté. Faites
chauffer de l'huile dans une grande poêle, placez les homards dedans, chair contre le fond,
et laissez-les séjourner pendant quelques minutes jusqu'à ce que la chair soit bien saisie et
qu'elle commence à prendre couleur. Sortez
les homards de la poêle et saupoudrez-les avec
le sel, la poudre de cardamome verte, le
sucre, la coriandre verte et faites goutter le
lait de noix de coco dessus. Placez chaque
demi-homard sous le gril et servez une fois
cuit (normalement, 8 à 10 minutes suffisent
pour obtenir un bon résultat). Quant à la pince :
faites chauffer l'huile dans une poêle, ajoutez
les oignons et faites les sauter jusqu'à ce
qu'ils soient très bien dorés, ajoutez la pince
du homard et mélangez fréquemment à feu vif.
Ajoutez le gingembre et faites sauter le tout
pendant deux minutes de plus environ en ajou-
tant les tomates et en faisant cuire jusqu'à ce
que le mélange ne comporte plus de liquide.
Ajoutez le sel, vérifiez la consistance et servez
ce mélange dans la tête du homard.

2 bogavantes, cortados por la mitad a lo
largo. Pida en la pescadería que se los
preparen así. Abrir la pinza y reservar la
carne.
1 cucharadita de aceite vegetal o de maíz
1 cucharadita de sal
1 cucharadita de cardamomo verde en
polvo
1 cucharadita de azúcar
El zumo de un limón
20 g de cilantro picado
1 cucharadita de leche de coco

Para la carne de la pinza:
1 cucharadita de aceite
1 cebolla picada fina
1 trozo (2,5 cm) de jengibre picado fino
1 tomate mediano picado en cubitos
1 cucharadita de chile en polvo
1 cucharadita de sal

Limpie y seque bien los bogavantes.
Resérvelos. Caliente el aceite en una sartén grande, coloque los bogavantes con el
lado de la carne hacia abajo y dórelos bien
a fuego alto. Retírelos de la sartén y agré-
gueles sal, cardamomo verde, azúcar, cilantro y riéguelos con la leche de coco.
Colóquelos en la parrilla y áselos hasta
que estén cocidos (de 8 a 10 minutos
debería ser suficiente). Para preparar la
carne de la pinza caliente el aceite en una
sartén, agregue la cebolla y saltéela hasta
que dore. A continuación agregue la carne
y fríala rápidamente a fuego alto. Agregue
el jengibre y saltee otro par de minutos.
Incorpore los tomates y cuézalos hasta
que la mezcla se seque. Agregue sal, veri-
fique la consistencia y sirva en la cabeza
del bogavante.

Eat and two veg

Design: Gabriel Murry
Proprietor: David Krantz, Chaker Hanna
Headchef: Andrew Abrams | General Manager: Paul Wood

50 Marylebone High Street | Marylebone W1U 5HN
Phone: +44 20 7258 8595
www.eatandtwoveg.com, info@eatandtwoveg.com
Tube: Baker Street
Opening hours: Mon–Fri 8 am to 11 pm, Sat 9 am to 11 pm, Sun 10 am to 10 pm
Average price £21
Cuisine: Vegetarian

EightOverEight

Design: Chris Connell | Chef: Neil Whitney

392 King's Road | Chelsea, SW3 5UZ
Phone: +44 20 7349 9934
Tube: Sloane Square
Opening hours: Lunch Mon–Fri 12 noon to 3 pm, Sat 12 noon to 4 pm,
Sun 1 pm to 4 pm, dinner Mon–Sat 6 pm to 11 pm, Sun 6 pm to 10:30 pm
Average price: £35
Cuisine: Asian

Chilli Salt Squid
with sweet chilli sauce

Kalmar mit süßer Chilisoße
Encornet au sel et au chilli avec une sauce douce au chilli
Calamar con salsa dulce de chile

Chilli sauce:
4 1/2 oz large red chilli de-seeded
2 1/3 oz garlic, thinly sliced
310 ml distilled white vinegar
1/2 lb 3 oz white sugar
Fish sauce to taste
1 spring onion

Place vinegar, sugar and red chilli in saucepan and reduce down to syrup. Add fish sauce to taste.

Squid:
Clean the squid and slice very finely (almost shaved) at an angle. Cover well with cornflour (make sure every part of squid is covered). Leave to stand then cover with cornflour again. Fry the squid, season with salt and freshly cracked pepper and finish with julienne of spring onion and chopped red chilli.

Chilisauce:
125 g große rote Chilischote, entkernt
65 g Knoblauch, dünn geschnitten
310 ml weißer Essig, destilliert
310 g weißer Zucker
Fischsoße nach Geschmack
1 Frühlingszwiebel

Essig, Zucker und rote Chilischote in einen Soßentopf geben und solange köcheln, bis ein Sirup entsteht. Fügen sie Fischsoße hinzu, je nach Geschmack.

Kalmar:
Reinigen Sie den Kalmar und schneiden Sie ihn in sehr dünne Scheiben. In Mehl wenden und darauf achten, dass alle Teile gut bedeckt sind. Kurz ruhen lassen und anschließend erneut in Mehl wenden. Den Kalmar anbraten, mit Salz und frisch gemahlenem Pfeffer würzen. Anschließend mit Julienne-Frühlingszwiebeln und gehacktem roten Chili garnieren.

Sauce au chilli :
125 g de chillis rouges égrenés
65 g d'ail coupé en tranches fines
310 ml de vinaigre blanc distillé
310 g de sucre blanc
Fumet de poisson pour parfaire le goût
1 oignon vert

Placez le vinaigre, le sucre et le chilli rouge dans une casserole et réduisez jusqu'à obtention d'un sirop. Ajoutez le fumet de poisson pour harmoniser le goût.

Encornet :
Nettoyez l'encornet et découpez-le en tranches très fines inclinées (presque comme si vous rasiez la surface). Couvrez bien avec la farine de maïs (assurez-vous que toute la chair de l'encornet est entièrement recouverte de liquide). Laissez reposer puis recouvrez à nouveau. Faites frire l'encornet, assaisonnez avec du sel et du poivre que vous venez de moudre, puis ajoutez pour terminer une julienne d'oignon et du chilli rouge découpé en tranches.

Para la salsa:
125 g de guindilla roja picada y sin semillas
65 g de ajo, tajado fino
310 ml de vinagre blanco
310 g de azúcar
Salsa de pescado para condimentar
1 cebolleta

Ponga el vinagre, el azúcar y la guindilla a cocer en un cazo hasta que alcance el punto de almíbar. Condimente con la salsa de pescado.

Calamar:
Limpie y corte finamente el calamar al sezgo. Páselo por harina (asegurarse de que todas las partes queden cubiertas). Déjelo reposar y páselo nuevamente por harina. Fria el calamar, salpimiéntelo y sírvalo con julianas de cebolleta y guindilla roja picada.

E&O

Design: Chris Connell | Owner: Will Ricker
Chef: Simon Treadway

14 Blenheim Crescent | Notting Hill Gate, W11 1NN
Phone: +44 20 7229 5454
Tube: Ladbroke Grove, Notting Hill Gate
Opening hours: Lunch Mon–Fri 12:15 pm to 3 pm, Sat 12:15 pm to 4 pm,
Sun 1 pm to 4 pm, dinner Mon–Sat 6:15 pm to 10:30 pm, Sun 6:15 pm to 10 pm
Average price: £32
Cuisine: Asian

Daikon Salad

Daikonsalat (japanischer weißer Rettich)
Salade de daikon (radis blanc d'Asie)
Ensalada Daikon (rábano japonés)

Daikon sheet cut using a Japanese sheet mandolin
Mixed salad leaves
Avocado
Crispy shallots
Red peppers
Enoki mushrooms
Chives

Make the rolls using the sheets filled with all the other ingredients.

400 ml grapeseed oil
300 ml Sushi vinegar
8 3/4 oz Daikon
5 cloves garlic
1 3/4 oz peeled ginger
1 3/4 oz peeled shallots
50 ml soy sauce
Sugar and lime juice to taste

Blend all together until smooth.

Daikon Blätter, geschnitten mit einer japanischen Mandoline
Salatblätter, gemischt
Avocado
Schalotten, knackig frisch
Rote Paprika
Enoki Pilze
Schnittlauch

Die Blätter mit den anderen Zutaten füllen und rollen.

400 ml Traubenkernöl
300 ml Sushi-Essig
250 g Daikon (weißer japanischer Rettich)
5 Knoblauchzehen
50 g Ingwer, geschält
50 g Schalotten, geschält
50 ml Sojasoße
Zucker und Limettensaft nach Geschmack

Alle Zutaten gut verrühren.

Feuilles de daikon coupée à l'aide d'un
« mandoline » à feuilles japonais
Feuilles de salades mixtes
Avocat
Echalotes croustillantes
Poivron rouge
Champignons enoki
Ciboulette

Faites des roulés en vous servant des
feuilles garnies avec tous les autres ingrédients cités.

400 ml d'huile de grains de raisins
300 ml de vinaigre à sushi
250 g de daikon
5 gousses d'ail
50 g de gingembre pelé
50 g d'échalotes pelées
50 ml de sauce au soja
Sucre et jus de lime selon vos goûts

Mélangez le tout jusqu'à obtention d'une
consistance homogène.

Hojas de daikon cortadas con una mandoli-
na japonesa
Variedad de lechugas
Aguacate
Chalotes tostados
Pimientos rojos
Setas enoki
Cebollino

Rellene las hojas de daikon con el resto de
los ingredientes y arme los rollitos.

400 ml de aceite de semillas de uva
300 ml de vinagre para sushi
250 g de daikon
5 dientes de ajo
50 g de jengibre pelado
50 g de chalotes pelados
50 ml de salsa de soya
Azúcar y zumo de lima al gusto

Mezcle hasta que la consistencia sea
homogénea.

Fifth Floor

Design: Lifschutz Davidson I Chef: Simon Shaw

109–125 Knightsbridge I Knightsbridge, SW1X 7RJ
Phone: +44 20 7235 5250
www.harveynichols.com
Tube: Knightsbridge
Opening hours: Lunch Mon–Fri 12 noon to 3 pm, Sat–Sun 12 noon to 3:30 pm,
dinner Mon–Sat 6 pm to 11 pm
Average price: £38
Cuisine: British (Modern)

Timbale

of Cantabrian anchovies with new potato salad, apple, cucumber and ginger dressing

Timbale aus kantabrischen Anchovis mit Salat aus neuen Kartoffeln, Apfel und Gurke mit Ingwer-Dressing
Timbale d'anchois de la Cantabrique, accompagnée d'une salade de pommes de terre nouvelles à la pomme et au concombre ainsi que d'une sauce au gingembre
Timbal de anchoas Cantábricas con ensalada de patatas nuevas, pepino y manzana con guarnición de jengibre

1 small tin Cantabrian anchovies
7 oz peeled new potatoes
1 oz diced banana shallots
2¹/₂ oz mayonnaise
¹/₃ oz chopped chives
100 ml crème fraiche
Zest and juice of lemon
1 cucumber (peeled)
1 apple
100 ml apple and ginger juice
²/₃ oz apple pectin
¹/₆ oz smoked paprika
¹/₃ oz Oscietra caviar
Four stainless steel rings for building the timbale

Boil potatoes and refresh with cold water. Cut into small dice, add chopped shallots and bind together with mayonnaise. Complete with chopped chives. Remove anchovies from the oil and lay on a paper towel. Line the ring with anchovies until they meet. Fill centre with potato salad, leaving a small gap on the top. Add lemon to crème fraiche, place on top and level to a smooth finish. Place a dab of caviar in centre.
Scoop cucumber into balls with small melon baller and cut apples into small cubes. For dressing, warm apple and ginger juice. Mix with apple pectin to form a syrup. Add the apple cubes and cucumber balls.
Use dressing to garnish the anchovies.

1 kleine Dose kantabrischer Anchovis
200 g neue Kartoffeln, geschält
25 g Bananen-Schalotten, gewürfelt
75 g Mayonnaise
10 g Schnittlauch, geschnitten
100 ml Crème Fraîche
Zitronenschale und -saft
1 Gurke, geschält
1 Apfel
100 ml Apfel- und Ingwersaft
20 g Apfelpektin
6 g geräucherte Paprika
10 g Oscietra Kaviar
Vier Edelstahl-Ringe zum Formen der Timbale

Kartoffeln kochen und mit kaltem Wasser abschrecken. In kleine Würfel schneiden, die gewürfelten Schalotten hinzugeben und beide Zutaten mit Mayonnaise binden. Mit dem geschnittenen Schnittlauch abrunden. Das Öl von den Anchovis abgießen und die Anchovis auf Küchenpapier legen. Den Ring so mit Anchovis belegen, dass sie eng aneinander liegen. In die Mitte den Kartoffelsalat geben und oben eine kleine Aussparung lassen. Crème Fraîche und Zitrone verrühren und darüber geben, gleichmäßig verteilen und in die Mitte einen Klacks Kaviar setzen.
Aus der Gurke mit einem kleinen Kugelausstecher Kugeln formen und den Apfel in kleine Würfel schneiden. Für das Dressing den Apfel- und Ingwersaft anwärmen. Mit dem Apfelpektin vermischen, damit sich ein Sirup bildet, die Apfelwürfel und die Gurkenkugeln hinzufügen.
Die Anchovis mit dem Dressing garnieren.

1 petite boîte d'anchois de Cantabrique
200 g de pommes de terre nouvelles pelées
75 g de mayonnaise
10 g de ciboulette hachée
100 ml de crème fraîche
Le zeste et le jus d'un citron
1 concombre (pelé)
1 pomme
100 ml de jus de pomme et de gingembre
20 g de pectine de pomme
5 g de poivron fumé
10 g de caviar Oscietra
Quatre ramequins en acier inox pour former la timbale

Faites bouillir les pommes de terre puis plongez-les dans l'eau froide. Découpez-les en petits dés, ajoutez les échalotes hachées puis liez le tout avec la mayonnaise. Complétez avec la ciboulette hachée. Retirez les anchois de leur huile et égouttez-les sur une serviette en papier. Garnissez les parois du ramequin avec les anchois jusqu'à ce qu'ils se rejoignent. Remplissez le centre avec la salade de pommes de terre en laissant une petite cavité au sommet. Ajoutez le citron à la crème fraîche, versez cette crème dans la cavité et lissez pour obtenir une surface plane. Ajoutez un soupçon de caviar au centre.
A l'aide d'une petite cuiller parisienne, découpez le concombre en petites boulettes, découpez aussi la pomme en petits cubes. Pour préparer la sauce, faites chauffer le jus de pomme et de gingembre. Mélangez-le avec la pectine de pomme pour obtenir un sirop. Ajoutez les petits cubes de pomme et les boulettes de concombre.
Versez la sauce sur les anchois pour les en garnir.

1 lata pequeña de anchoas cantábricas
200 g de patatas nuevas, peladas
25 g de chalotes alargados, picados
75 g de mayonesa
10 g de cebollino, cortado
100 ml de crème fraîche
Zumo y cáscara de limón
1 pepino, pelado
1 manzana
100 ml de zumo de manzana y jengibre
20 g de pectina de manzana
6 g de pimiento ahumado
10 g de caviar Oscietra
Cuatro anillos de acero fino para formar el timbal

Cocer las patatas y pasar por agua fría. Cortar en cuadraditos, añadir los chalotes picados y ligar con la mayonesa. Agregar el cebollino cortado. Separar el aceite de las anchoas y ponerlas sobre papel de cocina. Recubrir el anillo con las anchoas acomodadas una al lado de otra. Poner la ensalada de patatas en el centro y dejar un pequeño hueco en el centro. Mezclar la crème fraîche y el limón, verter encima y alisar. En el centro, colocar una pequeña cantidad de caviar.
Formar bolitas de pepino con el aparato correspondiente y cortar la manzana en cuadraditos. Para la guarnición, calentar el zumo de manzana y jengibre. Añadir la pectina de manzana para que se forme un almíbar. Luego agregar la manzana troceada y las bolitas de pepino.
Guarnecer las anchoas con el aderezo.

Fifteen

Design: Bluearc | Chef: Jamie Oliver

15 Westland Place | Shoreditch | Spitalfields, N1 7LP
Phone: +44 871 333 1515
www.fifteenrestaurant.com
Tube: Old Street
Opening hours: Lunch 12 noon to 3 pm, dinner 7 pm to 11 pm
Average price: £55
Cuisine: Mediterranean

Christmas Salad

Weihnachtssalat
Salade de Noël
Ensalada de Navidad

12 slices of Speck
A bunch of watercress
A bunch of white dandelion or rocket
A few leaves of treviso
4 clementines
Good balsamic vinegar
Good olive oil
Parmesan cheese

Trim and wash the watercress if it needs it
and with a pair of scissors, trim the dandelion or rocket and add it to the same bowl
with the treviso. Carefully peel the clementines, keeping them whole, and slice them
into thin slices.
Add the sliced clementines to the salad
leaves and dress with olive oil, a splash of
balsamic vinegar, salt and pepper.
Divide the salad between four plates and
tuck 3 pieces of Speck in amongst the
salad leaves. Shave a few pieces of
Parmesan cheese over the top and drizzle
with a little more balsamic vinegar and
some extra virgin olive oil.

12 Scheiben Speck
Einen Bund Brunnenkresse
Einen Bund Löwenzahn oder Rucola
Ein paar Blätter Treviso-Salat
4 Klementinen
Balsamico, hochwertig
Olivenöl, hochwertig
Parmesankäse

Die Brunnenkresse waschen und gegebe-
nenfalls stutzen. Anschließend den Löwenzahn oder den Rucola mit einer Schere zu-
rechtschneiden und mit dem Treviso-Salat
in eine Schüssel geben. Die Klementinen
vorsichtig schälen, ohne sie zu beschä-
digen. Dann in dünne Scheiben schneiden.
Die Klementinenscheiben mit den Salatblättern vermischen, mit Olivenöl anmachen, einen Schuss Balsamico-Essig hinzufügen und mit Salz und Pfeffer würzen.
Den Salat auf vier Teller verteilen und
jeweils 3 Scheiben Speck zwischen den
Salatblättern anrichten. Ein wenig Parmesankäse darüber reiben und mit ein paar
Tropfen Balsamico-Essig und Olivenöl
beträufeln.

12 tranches de lard
Un bouquet de cresson d'eau
Un bouquet de pissenlits blancs ou de
roquette
Quelques feuilles de trévise
4 clémentines
Un bon vinaigre balsamique
Une huile d'olive de bonne qualité
Parmesan

Ecourtez et lavez le cresson d'eau si
nécessaire, et, avec une paire de ciseaux,
écourtez aussi les pissenlits ou la roquette
et mettez ensuite leurs feuilles dans le
même saladier que la trévise. Pelez
soigneusement les clémentines en veillant
à les laisser entières, puis découpez-les en
tranches minces.
Ajoutez les clémentines ainsi émincées
aux feuilles de salade et apprêtez avec
l'huile d'olive, un jet de vinaigre balsamique, du sel et du poivre.
Répartissez la salade sur quatre assiettes
et, sur chaque, placez 3 morceaux de lard
dans les feuilles de salade. Parsemez le
parmesan sur le tout puis versez un filet
supplémentaire de vinaigre balsamique et
d'huile d'olive vierge extra.

12 lonchas de beicon
Un ramo de berros
Un ramo de diente de león o de rúcola
Unas cuantas hojas de chicoria trevisana
4 clementinas
Vinagre balsámico de buena calidad
Aceite de oliva de buena calida
Queso parmesano

Corte y lave, si es necesario, los berros y
con unas tijeras corte el diente de león o
la rúcola y póngalos junto con las hojas de
chicoria en una ensaladera. Pele con cui-
dado las clementinas, dejándolas enteras y
luego tájelas en rodajas finas.
Agregue las rodajas de clementina a la
ensalada y aderece con aceite de oliva, un
chorrito de vinagre balsámico, sal y
pimienta.
Reparta la ensalada en cuatro platos y
mezcle entre las hojas de la ensalada tres
trozos de beicon. Ralle encima un poco de
queso parmesano y rocíe con un poco de
balsámico y de aceite de oliva.

Hakkasan

Design: Jestico + Whiles, Christian Liaigre
Chef: Tong Chee Hwee | Owner: Alan Yau

8 Hanway Place | Bloomsbury, W1 P9HD
Phone: +44 20 7927 7000
Tube: Tottenham Court Road
Opening hours: Mon–Sun 12 noon to 3 pm & 6 pm to 12 midnight
Average price: £40
Cuisine: Dim Sum, Chinese

Isola

Design: Andy Martin | Owner: Oliver Peyton
Chef: Mark Broadbent

145 Knightsbridge | Knightsbridge, SW1X 7PA
Phone: +44 20 7838 1055
Tube: Knightsbridge
Opening hours: Mon–Sat 12 noon to 2:45 pm & 6 pm to 10:45 pm
Average price: £40
Cuisine: Italian (Contemporary)

Locanda Locatelli

Design: David Collins | Chef: Giorgio Locatelli

8 Seymour Street | Marylebone, W1H 7JZ
Phone: +44 20 7935 9088
www.locandalocatelli.com | info@locandalocatelli.com
Tube: Marble Arch
Opening hours: Mon–Sat 12 noon to 3 pm & 7 pm to 11 pm
Average price: £45
Cuisine: Italian (Contemporary)

Coniglio al Forno

con prosciutto crudo e polenta

Rabbit with Parma ham and polenta
Geschmortes Kaninchen mit Parmaschinken und Polenta
Lapin au four, au jambon crû et à la polenta
Conejo al horno con jamón de Parma y polenta

6 rabbit legs, boned
12 thin slices of Parma ham
2 tbsp groundnut oil
2 oz butter
1 lb 2 oz lard, melted
4 oz polenta
2 pints milk
2 heads of radicchio Trevisano
Sea salt and freshly ground pepper

Preheat the oven to 120 °C (258 °F), Gas Mark 1.5. Wrap each rabbit leg in 2 slices of Parma ham. Heat half the oil in a large shallow casserole and place the rabbit legs in it. Fry over a medium heat until they start to color, then add the butter. Turn the legs over and cook for a further 2 minutes. Cover the legs completely with the melted lard, then cover with foil and cook very gently in the oven for 1 hour, until very tender.
Meanwhile, cook the polenta. Put it in a large jug so that it can be poured in a steady stream. Bring the milk to the boil in a large saucepan; it should half fill the pan. Add 1 teaspoon of salt and then slowly add the polenta in a continuous stream, stirring with a long-handled whisk all the time, until completely blended. The polenta will start to bubble volcanically. Reduce the heat as low as possible and cook for 20 minutes, stirring occasionally. Cut each raddichio into 3 and season with salt and pepper. Brush with the remaining oil and cook on a medium-hot griddle pan, until wilted. Spoon the polenta on to 6 serving plates and put the rabbit legs on top. Add the raddichio to the side and serve straight away.

6 Kaninchenkeulen, mit Knochen
12 dünne Scheiben Parmaschinken
2 EL Erdnussöl
50 g Butter
500 g Schweinefett, geschmolzen
125 g Polenta
1,2 l Milch
2 Köpfe Radicchio di Treviso
Meersalz und frisch gemahlenen Pfeffer

Den Ofen auf 120 °C, Gas 1,5 vorheizen. Die Kaninchenkeulen in 2 Scheiben Parmaschinken einwickeln. Die Hälfte des Öls in einer flachen Kasserolle erhitzen und die Kaninchenkeulen hineinlegen. Bei mittlerer Hitze braten, bis sie anfangen, Farbe anzunehmen. Dann die Butter hinzufügen, die Keulen wenden und weitere zwei Minuten braten. Anschließend mit dem zerlassenen Schweinefett bedecken. Das Ganze mit einer Folie abdecken und bei mittlerer Hitze für eine Stunde im Ofen schmoren lassen, bis die Keulen zart werden. Währenddessen die Polenta kochen. Schütten Sie die Polenta in einen großen Behälter, um sie von dort aus in einem Strahl der Milch zugeben zu können. Die Milch in einem großen Soßentopf kochen, wobei dieser nur zur Hälfte gefüllt sein sollte. Einen Teelöffel Salz dazugeben und dann langsam und gleichmäßig die Polenta in die Milch schütten. Mit einem Schneebesen so lange umrühren, bis alles vermischt ist. Die Polenta wird anfangen stark zu blubbern, deshalb bei schwacher Hitze, unter gelegentlichem Umrühren, 20 Minuten kochen lassen. Jedes Radicchio in 3 Teile schneiden und mit Salz und Pfeffer würzen. Mit dem übrigen Öl bestreichen und bei mittelschwacher Hitze auf einem Backblech garen, bis der Radicchio eingefallen ist. Die Polenta gleichmäßig auf 6 Teller verteilen und die Kaninchenkeulen darauf platzieren. Den Radicchio daneben legen und sofort servieren.

6 cuisses de lapin avec leur os
12 fines tranches de jambon de Parme
2 c. à soupe d'huile de graine d'arachide
50 g de beurre
500 g de saindoux
125 g de polenta
1,2 litre de lait
2 cœurs de trévise
Sel de mer et poivre fraîchement moulu

Préchauffez le four à 120 °C, graduation 1,5 sur un four à gaz. Enveloppez chaque cuisse de lapin dans deux tranches de jambon de Parme. Faites chauffer la moitié de l'huile dans une grande casserole peu profonde et placez les cuisses dedans. Faites rissoler à feu moyen jusqu'à ce que le jambon commence à prendre de la couleur, puis ajoutez le beurre. Retournez les cuisses puis poursuivez la cuisson pendant 2 minutes supplémentaires. Recouvrez entièrement les cuisses avec le saindoux fondu, puis recouvrez avec une feuille d'aluminium et poursuivez la cuisson pendant 1 heure, au four réglé très bas, jusqu'à ce que la chair du lapin soit très tendre.
Dans une grande casserole, faites bouillir le lait ; il faudrait qu'il la remplisse à moitié. Ajoutez 1 c. à café de sel puis incorporez lentement la polenta en la faisant couler continuellement et tout en mélangeant tout le temps avec un fouet à manche long, jusqu'à obtention d'une consistance homogène. La polenta se met à bouillir à gros bouillons. Réduisez le feu au maximum et faites cuire pendant 20 minutes en mélangeant de temps en temps. Coupez chacune des deux trévises en 3 puis assaisonnez-la avec le sel et le poivre. Essuyez l'huile restante et faites cuire dans une galettière mi-chaude jusqu'à ce que les feuilles soient flétries. A la cuillère, versez la polenta dans 6 assiettes de service et mettez les cuisses de lapin par dessus. Disposez la trévise sur le côté et servez immédiatement.

6 piernas de conejo con hueso
12 tajadas finas de jamón de Parma
2 cucharadas de aceite de maní
50 g de mantequilla
500 g de manteca de cerdo, derretida
125 g de polenta
1.2 l de leche
2 cabezas de chicoria trevisana
Sal marina y pimienta fresca molida

Precalentar el horno a 120 °C, gas 1.5. Envuelva cada pierna de conejo con dos tajadas de jamón de parma. Caliente la mitad del aceite en una cacerola poco profunda y fría a fuego medio las piernas hasta que empiecen a tomar color. Añada la mantequilla. Déles la vuelta a las piernas y cueza otros dos minutos. Unte bien las piernas con la manteca derretida, cúbralas con papel de aluminio y cuézalas en el horno durante una hora, hasta que estén tiernas.
Entretanto prepare la polenta. Póngala en un recipiente desde donde la pueda verter de manera constante. Ponga la leche a hervir en una olla grande, más o menos debe llenar media olla. Agregue una cucharadita de sal e incorpore poco a poco la polenta, de forma continua, revolviendo con un batidor de mano hasta que esté completamente mezclada. La polenta empezará a hacer burbujas. Baje el fuego al mínimo y cueza 20 minutos, mezclando de vez en cuando. Corte cada chicoria en tres y condimente con sal y pimienta. Úntelas con el aceite restante y áselas a la plancha a fuego medio hasta que se marchiten. Sirva la polenta en cada plato y coloque el conejo encima. Sirva la chicoria al lado como guarnición y sirva inmediatamente.

Momo and Kemia Bar

Design: Mourad Mazouz (Owner)
Executive Chef: Mohamed Ourad

25 Heddon Street | London W1B 4BH
Phone: +44 20 7434 4040
Tube: Piccadilly Circus, Oxford Circus
Opening hours: Lunch Mon–Sat 12 noon to 2:30 pm, dinner Mon–Sun 7 pm to
11:30 pm
Average price (without wine): £36
Cuisine: North African

Momo Special

Take a bunch of fresh mint leaves.
Shake them with ice cubes in a cocktail
shaker to allow the aroma of the mint to
break out.
Add 50 ml of vodka, 10 ml of freshly
squeezed lemon juice and 10 ml of syrup
of gomme (sugared water).
Shake all the ingredients together.
Pour into glass over crushed ice and top
up with soda water.
Decorate with mint.

Einen Bund frischer Minzblätter mit
Eiswürfel in einem Cocktailshaker schüt-
teln, um das Aroma der Minze freizusetzen.
50 ml Vodka, 10 ml frisch gepressten
Limettensaft und 10 ml Gomme-Sirup
(Zuckerwasser) hinzufügen.
Alle Zutaten schütteln und in ein Glas mit
frisch gestoßenem Eis eingießen.
Mit Soda auffüllen und mit Minze
dekorieren.

Prenez un bouquet de feuilles de menthe
fraîche. Dans un coquetellier, agitez-les
avec des glaçons pour que l'arôme de la
menthe s'épanouisse.
Ajoutez 50 ml de vodka, 10 ml du jus d'un
citron pressé à l'instant et 10 ml de sirop
de gomme (eau sucrée).
Au coquetellier, agitez l'ensemble de ces
ingrédients.
Versez le cocktail dans un verre sur de la
glace pilée et recouvrez de soda.
Décorez avec des feuilles de menthe.

Agitar un manojo de hojas frescas de
menta con cubitos de hielo en una coctel-
era, para que se libere el aroma de la
menta.
Añadir 50 ml vodka, 10 ml de zumo fresco
de lima y 10 ml de jarabe de Gomme
(agua azucarada).
Agitar todos los ingredientes y verter en
un vaso con hielo recién triturado.
Añadir soda y decorar con hojas de menta.

Nobu

Design: United Designers | Executive Chef: Nobuyuki Matsuhisa
Head Chef London: Mark Edwards

19 Old Park Lane | Mayfair, W1Y 4LB
Phone: +44 20 7447 4747
www.noburestaurants.com
Tube: Oxford Circus, Hyde Park Corner
Opening hours: Lunch Mon–Fri 12 noon to 2:15 pm, dinner Mon–Fri 6 pm to
10:15 pm, Sat 6 pm to 11:15 pm, Sun 6 pm to 9:45 pm
Average price: £57
Cuisine: modern Japanese

Black Cod

with sweet Miso

Schwarzer Kabeljau mit süßem Miso
Morue charbonnière au miso doux
Bacalao negro con miso dulce

4 black cod fillets (pacific Sable fish)
around 1 kg total weight
Den Miso
4 stalk hajikami (pickled ginger stem)
4 slices of lemon

Den Miso
Sake
165 ml sweet sake (mirin)
1 lb 2 oz white miso paste
8½ oz granulated sugar

Bring the sake and mirin to a boil for
about 1 minute, add sugar and stir until
dissolved. Whisk in miso paste a little at
a time until sauce becomes smooth.
Cook in a double boiler for around 30
minutes and cool and reserve a small
amount for garnishing.
Place Sable fish into the rest of the cool
miso and refrigerate for 3 days.
Place fillets under grill and cook slowly
until the outside of the fish begins to
caramelize and turn golden brown
(around 15 minutes) and then finish off in
a hot oven for a further 5 minutes or until
cooked through. Serve with lemon slices
and a little of the reserved miso.

4 schwarze Kabeljaufilets (pazifischer
Zobel), ca. 1 kg Gesamtgewicht
Den Miso
4 Stängel Hajikami (eingelegte
Ingwerwurzeln)
4 Zitronenscheiben

Den Miso
Sake
165 ml süßer Sake (Mirin)
500 g weiße Misopaste
245 g Kristallzucker

Den Sake und den Mirin eine Minute lang
kochen. Zucker hinzufügen und so lange
umrühren, bis er sich vollkommen aufgelöst hat. Die Misopaste ein wenig umrühren, bis sie cremig wird. Ca. 30 Minuten
im Wasserbad kochen, abkühlen lassen
und eine kleine Menge zur Garnierung beiseite stellen.
Den Zobel in den gekühlten Miso legen und
drei Tage im Kühlschrank aufbewahren.
Die Filets auf kleiner Flamme grillen, bis
die Außenseite anfängt zu karamellisieren
und goldbraun wird (ca. 15 Minuten). Zum
Schluss weitere 5 Minuten – oder bis der
Fisch gar ist – auf großer Flamme grillen.
Mit Zitronenscheiben und dem restlichen
Miso servieren.

4 filets de morue (morue charbonnière du Pacifique), d'un poids total d'un kg env.
Den Miso
4 tiges d'hajikami (tige de gingembre marinée)
4 tranches de citron

Den Miso
Saké
165 ml de saké doux (mirin)
500 g de pâte de miso blanche
245 g de sucre granulé

Faites bouillir le saké et le mirin pendant env. 1 minute, ajoutez le sucre et mélangez jusqu'à dissolution complète.
Incorporez très progressivement la pâte de miso jusqu'à ce que la sauce devienne onctueuse. Faites cuire au bain-marie pendant env. 30 minutes puis laissez refroidir et réservez-en une petite quantité pour la garniture.
Placez la morue charbonnière dans le reste du miso froid et mettez-la au réfrigérateur pendant 3 jours.
Mettez les filets sous le gril et faites-les cuire doucement (pendant env. 15 minutes) jusqu'à que la partie extérieure du poisson commence à caraméliser et prenne une couleur très dorée. Achevez la cuisson dans un four très chaud, pendant 5 minutes, jusqu'à que la chair soit cuite à cœur. Servez avec les tranches de citron et un peu du miso que vous aviez réservé.

4 filetes de bacalao negro (bacalao del Pacífico), con un peso total de aprox. 1 kg
Den Miso
4 tallos de Hajikami (raíces de jenjibre macerado)
4 rodajas de limón

Den Miso
Sake
165 ml Sake dulce (Mirin)
500 g pasta de miso blanco
245 g azúcar granulado

Llevar el sake y el mirin a ebullición durante 1 minuto. Añadir el azúcar y remover hasta que se haya disuelto completamente. Remover ligeramente la pasta de miso hasta que obtenga una consistencia cremosa. Cocer aprox. 30 minutos al baño María, dejar enfriar y reservar una pequeña cantidad para la guarnición.
Colocar el bacalao del Pacífico en el miso frío y dejar reposar durante 3 días en el frigorífico.
Preparar los filetes a la brasa a fuego lento, hasta que la superficie del pescado empiece a caramelizar y adquiera un color dorado (aprox. 15 minutos). Finalmente, asarlos otros 5 minutos –o hasta que el pescado esté hecho– a fuego fuerte.
Servir con las rodajas de limón y el resto del miso.

Plateau

Design: Conran & Partners I Chef: Tim Tolley

4th Floor, Canada Place, Canary Wharf I Docklands, E14 4QS
Phone: +44 20 7715 7100
www.conran.com I plateau@conran-restaurants.co.uk
Tube: Canary Wharf
Opening hours: Restaurant lunch Mon–Fri 12 noon to 3 pm, dinner Mon–Fri 6
pm to 10:30 pm, Sat 6pm to 11pm I Bar & Grill Mon–Fri 12 noon to 11 pm,
Sat 11 am to 11 pm, Sun 11 am to 4 pm
Average price: £40
Cuisine: Modern French

Putney Bridge

Design: Paskin Kyriakides & Sands I Chef: Anthony Demetre

1 Embankment, Lower Richmond Road I Putney, SW15 1LB
Phone: +44 20 8780 1811
www.putneybridgerestaurant.com I reservations@putneybridgerestaurant.com
Tube: Putney Bridge
Opening hours: Mon–Sat 12 noon to 2 pm & 7 pm to 10:30 pm, Sun 12 noon to 3 pm
Average price: £45
Price range: Starters £8,50 – £16,50, main £17,50 – £22,50,
desert £6,50 – £10
Cuisine: French

Shumi

Design: United Designers, Keith Hobbs I Chef: Lee Purcell

23 St James's Street I St James's, SW1
Phone: +44 20 7747 9380
www.shumi-london.com
Tube: Green Park
Opening hours: Lunch Mon–Sat 12 noon to 3 pm, Sun 12 noon to 4 pm, dinner
Mon–Sat 5:30 pm to 11 pm
Average price: £55
Cuisine: Italian, Japanese

Sketch

Design: Mourad Mazouz, Gabban O'Keefe, Noe Duchaufour Lawrance, Marc Newson, Chris Levine & Vincent Le Roy
Executive chef: Pierre Gagnaire

9 Conduit Street | Mayfair, W1S 2XG
Phone: +44 870 777 4488
Tube: Oxford Circus
Opening hours: The Lecture Room and Library Tue–Sat 12 noon to 2 pm,
7 pm to 11 pm | The Gallery Mon–Sat 7 pm to 11 pm
Average price: The Gallery £40 | The Lecture Room and Library £125
Cuisine: New French

Spoon at Sanderson

Design: Philippe Starck | Chef: Alain Ducasse
Chef de cuisine: Pascal Feraud

50 Berners Street | Fitzrovia, W1T 3NG
Phone: +44 20 7300 1444
www.spoon-restaurant.com
Tube: Oxford Circus, Tottenham Court Road
Opening hours: Mon–Sun 12 noon to 3 pm, dinner Mon–Sun 6 pm to 11 pm
Average price: £50
Cuisine: Eclectic, Modern European

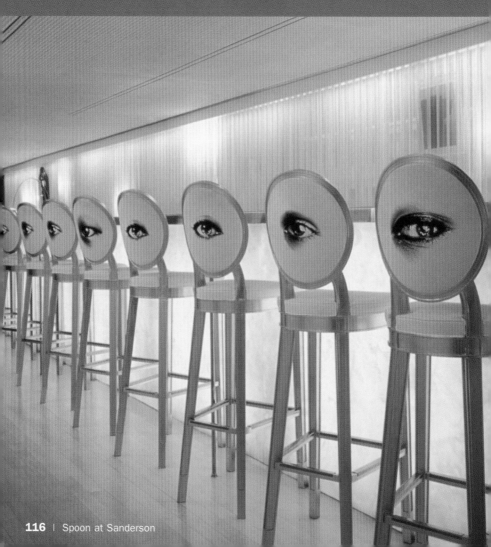

Spoon Ceviche

with "Grenobloise" condiment and mimosa garnish

Spoon Ceviche mit „Grenobloise"-Relish und Mimosa-Garnierung

Ceviche à la cuillère, avec condiment à la grenobloise et garniture mimosa

Ceviche con guarnición "Grenobloise" y acompañamiento mimosa

1 slice of white bread	1 Scheibe Weißbrot
1 red pepper	1 rote Paprika
1 green pepper	1 grüne Paprika
Juice of 2 limes	Saft zweier Limetten
1 chilli	1 Chilischote
1 shallot, finely sliced	1 Schalotte, in feine Scheiben geschnitten
1 garlic clove, finely chopped	1 Knoblauchzehe, fein gehackt
1½ lb 1¾ oz sea bass fillet, very fresh	800 g Wolfsbarschfilets, sehr frisch
sea salt, pepper	Meersalz, Pfeffer
For the Grenobloise Relish Sauce:	Für die Grenobloise Relish Soße:
1 oz butter	30 g Butter
1¾ oz capers	50 g Kapern
2 limes, divided into segments	2 Limetten, in Stückchen geschnitten
1 slice of white bread	1 Scheibe Weißbrot
For the Mimosa Garnish Accompaniment:	Für die Mimosa Garnish Beilagen:
2 hard boiled eggs	2 hart gekochte Eier
Small bunch of parsley	kleiner Bund Petersilie

Cut the crusts from the bread and cut into thin strips, fry in a little oil until pale golden brown, then transfer to a sieve to drain. Peel the peppers, discard the stalks, seeds and pith and dice finely. Add the lime juice, chilli, shallot and garlic. Add plenty of pepper. Trim the fish fillet, then cut it into 1 cm thick slices. Marinate each slice for only 10 seconds, just long enough to flavour it but not to "cook", unlike classic ceviche. Drain the fish then slice almost in half. Open out, like a book, and fill with the marinade, as a filling-cum-topping. Season with salt and pepper and garnish the plate with the mimosa. Serve the relish separately. Heat the butter until golden brown, add the capers and cook for 1–2 minutes, then add the lime segments. Divide equally among 4 little sauce bowls and sprinkle with the fried bread strips. Separate the egg yolks from the whites. Push the yolks through a fine sieve and the whites chop finely. Chop the parsley very finely. Arrange in separate lines on each plate.

Die Brotkruste abschneiden und in dünne Streifen schneiden. Das Brot in etwas Öl anbraten, bis es leicht goldbraun wird. Das Öl danach in einem Sieb ablassen. Die Paprika säubern und entkernen und in feine Würfel schneiden. Limettensaft, Chilischote, Schalotte, Knoblauch sowie ausreichend Pfeffer hinzufügen. Die Fischfilets säubern und in 1 cm dicke Stücke schneiden. Für den Geschmack, jedes Stück lediglich 10 Sekunden marinieren, jedoch nicht „kochen" wie beim klassischen Ceviche. Den Fisch abtupfen und in nicht ganz zwei Hälften schneiden. Wie ein Buch aufklappen und die Marinade einfüllen. Mit Salz und Pfeffer würzen und den Teller mit Mimosa garnieren. Das Relish separat servieren. Die Butter erhitzen, bis sie braun wird und die Kapern darin 1–2 Minuten dünsten. Anschließend die Limettenstückchen hinzufügen und alles gleichmäßig auf 4 kleine Suppenschüsseln verteilen und mit den gerösteten Brotstreifen bestreuen. Das Eigelb vom Eiweiß trennen und durch ein feines Sieb passieren. Das Eiweiß fein schneiden. Die Petersilie fein hacken. In separaten Linien auf dem Teller anrichten.

1 tranche de pain blanc
1 poivron rouge
1 poivron vert
Le jus de 2 limes, 1 chilli
1 échalote découpée en tranches fines
1 gousse d'ail hachée fine
800 g filet de bar, très frais
Sel de mer, Poivre
Condiment à la grenobloise sauce :
30 g de beurre, 50 g de câpres
2 limes partagées en segments
1 tranche de pain blanc
Garniture mimosa accompagnement :
2 œufs cuits durs, 1 petit bouquet de persil

Détachez la croûte du pain et découpez-le en
bandes fines, faites-les frire dans un peu d'huile
jusqu'à ce qu'elles soient légèrement dorées,
puis transférez-les dans un tamis pour qu'elles
s'égouttent. Pelez les piments, enlevez les
pédoncules, les graines et la chair centrale
puis découpez-les en dés fins. Ajoutez le jus de
la lime, le chilli, les échalotes et l'ail. Saupoudrez généreusement de poivre. Lavez le filet de
poisson puis découpez-le en tranches épaisses
d'env. 1 cm. Faites mariner chaque tranche
pendant 10 secondes, temps nécessaire à ce
que le filet prenne un peu de la saveur, mais
insuffisant pour qu'il « cuise » comme dans un
ceviche classique. Egouttez le poisson puis
partagez-le presque en deux. Ouvrez-le en deux
avec un couteau, comme un livre, et versez
dedans la marinade à titre à la fois de farce et
de garniture. Assaisonnez avec le sel et le
poivre puis garnissez le plat avec la garniture
mimosa. Servez le condiment séparément.
Faites chauffer le beurre jusqu'à ce qu'il dore,
ajoutez les câpres et faites-les cuire pendant
1–2 minutes, puis ajoutez les segments de
lime. Répartissez le condiment à parts égales
entre 4 petits ramequins et garnissez ensuite
avec les lanières de pain frites. Séparez les
jaunes des blancs. Passez les jaunes au tamis
fin et les blancs hachez finement. Hachez le
persil très fin. Disposez sous forme de lignes
séparées sur chaque assiette.

1 rebanada de pan blanco
1 pimiento rojo
1 pimiento verde
El zumo de 2 limones
1 chile
1 chalota cortada muy fina
1 diente de ajo cortado muy fino
800g de lubina
Sal marina, pimienta
Guarnición Grenobloise Salsa:
30 g de mantequilla
50 g de alcaparras
2 limas en gajos
1 rebanada de pan blanco
Guarnición Mimosa Acompañamiento:
2 huevos cocidos
Un ramillete de perejil

Retirar la corteza del pan y cortarlo en
tiras muy finas; freír con poco aceite hasta
que adquieran un color tostado claro y
poner a escurrir. Pelar los pimientos, retirar los tallos, semillas y nervios y cortar
en dados pequeños. Agregar el zumo de
lima, el chile, la chalota y el ajo. Añadir
bastante pimienta. Cortar el pescado en
rodajas de 1 cm de grosor. Marinar cada
rodaja durante sólo 10 segundos para que
adquieran sabor pero sin "cocinarse", a
diferencia del ceviche clásico. Escurrir el
pescado y cortarlo en forma de libro. Abrir
el libro y usar la marinada como relleno y
como cobertura. Salpimentar y guarnecer
el plato con el acompañamiento Mimosa.
Servir la salsa por separado. Calentar la
mantequilla hasta que esté dorada, agregar las alcaparras y cocinar durante 1–2
minutos; agregar luego los gajos de lima.
Dividir en 4 salseras iguales y acompañar
con las tiras de pan frito. Separar las
yemas y las claras de los huevos. Hacer
pasar las yemas a través de un colador de
malla fina y las claras cortar en trozos
pequeños. Cortar el perejil muy fino.
Disponer en filas separadas en cada plato.

Tom Aikens

Design: Anouska Hempel I Chef: Tom Aikens

43 Elystan Street I Chelsea, SW3 3NT
Phone: +44 20 7584 2003
Tube: South Kensington
Opening hours: Mon–Fri 12 noon to 2:30 pm, 7 pm to 11 pm
Average price: £70
Cuisine: New French

Roast Langoustines

with Jabugo ham and coco beans

Geröstete Garnelen mit Jabugo-Schinken und Kokosbohnen
Langoustines rôties au jambon de Jabugo et aux haricots coco
Cigalas asadas con jamón de Jabugo y alubias

10½ oz fresh coco beans
1 carrot, peeled and halved
1 onion, peeled and quartered
2 large shallots, peeled and quartered
5 oz smoked bacon
100 ml double cream
1¾ oz diced onion
1½ oz butter
1 sprig thyme
¾ oz diced Jabugo ham
4 large raw langoustines, peeled
2 slices Jabugo ham
Pea shoots dressed with a little vinaigrette
A little olive oil
Salt and pepper

300 g frische Kokosbohnen
1 Karotte, geschält und halbiert
1 Zwiebel, geschält und geviertelt
2 große Schalotten, geschält und geviertelt
150 g Räucherschinken
100 ml Schlagsahne
50 g Zwiebeln, gewürfelt
40 g Butter
1 Bund Thymian
25 g Jabugo-Schinken, gewürfelt
4 große rohe Garnelen, geschält
2 Scheiben Jabugo-Schinken
Zuckerschoten, leicht in Vinaigrette mariniert
Olivenöl, geringe Menge
Salz und Pfeffer

Bring the beans to the boil, drain, rinse with cold water and then put back in the pan with the carrot, onion, shallots and bacon. Cover with cold water and then simmer for 30 minutes, until tender. When cooked drain off the beans and reserve the cooking liquor. Take half the cooked beans and half the cooking liquor and bring to the boil with 50 ml double cream. Season with salt and pepper. Keep warm and froth lightly to serve. Cook the diced onion with ¾ oz butter and thyme on a low heat until cooked, but not colored. Remove the thyme and set aside. Seal the Jabugo ham in a little olive oil and add the cooked onion and remaining beans and 50 ml of the cooking liquor. Cook until thickened and then add 50 ml cream and ¾ oz butter. Gently stir together until the cream and butter are fully emulsified. In a hot pan, heat a little olive oil. Season the langoustines and then cook for 1 minute, turning once. Put a little of the beans on each plate, place the langoustine on top with the pea shoots and shreds of ham. Drizzle the bean sauce around.

Die Bohnen zum Kochen bringen, abschütten, mit kaltem Wasser abschrecken und mit der Karotte, der Zwiebel, den Schalotten und dem Schinken zurück in den Topf geben. Mit kaltem Wasser bedecken und 30 Minuten köcheln lassen, bis sie gar sind. Wenn die Bohnen gar sind, abschütten und den Saft aufbewahren. Die Hälfte der Bohnen und die Hälfte der Flüssigkeit mit 50 ml Schlagsahne zum Kochen bringen und mit Salz und Pfeffer würzen. Warm halten und vor dem Servieren ein wenig schaumig schlagen. Die gewürfelte Zwiebel mit 20 g Butter und Thymian bei schwacher Hitze kochen, bis sie gar, jedoch noch nicht braun ist. Den Thymian entnehmen und beiseite legen. Jabugo-Schinken in ein wenig Olivenöl dünsten. Die gekochte Zwiebel, die übrigen Bohnen und 50 ml der restlichen Flüssigkeit hinzufügen. Kochen lassen bis es dickflüssig wird, anschließend 50 ml Schlagsahne und 20 g Butter dazugeben. Leicht rühren bis sich Schlagsahne und Butter vollkommen aufgelöst haben. Ein wenig Olivenöl in einer heißen Pfanne erhitzen, die Garnelen würzen und eine Minute braten, dabei wenden. Die Bohnen auf dem Teller platzieren und daneben die Garnelen mit den Zuckerschoten und den Schinkenstückchen anordnen. Den Rand des Tellers mit der Bohnenpaste ausschmücken.

300 g de haricots coco frais
1 carotte pelée et partagée en deux
1 oignon pelé et partagé en quatre quarts
2 grosses échalotes pelées et coupées en quarts
150 g de bacon fumé
100 ml de crème double
50 g d'oignon coupé en dés
40 g de beurre
1 branche de thym
25 g de jambon de Jabugo coupé en dés
4 grandes langoustines crues pelées
2 tranches de jambon de Jabugo
Pousses de pois apprêtées avec un peu de vinaigrette
Un peu d'huile d'olive
Sel et poivre

Faites bouillir les haricots, égouttez et rincez-les à l'eau froide puis remettez-les dans la casserole avec les carottes, les oignons, les échalotes et le bacon. Recouvrez avec de l'eau froide puis laissez frémir pendant 30 minutes jusqu'à ce que les légumes soient tendres. Une fois cuits, égouttez les haricots et réservez le jus de cuisson. Prenez la moitié des haricots cuits et la moitié du jus de cuisson et faites les bouillir avec 50 ml de crème double. Assaisonnez avec le sel et le poivre. Maintenez au chaud et faites mousser légèrement pour servir. Faites cuire les dés d'oignon dans 20 g de beurre et avec le thym, à feu réduit, jusqu'à ce qu'ils soient cuits mais non dorés. Retirez le thym et mettez-le de côté. Recouvrez le jambon de Jabugo d'un peu d'huile d'olive et ajoutez les dés d'oignon cuits et les haricots restants, plus 50 ml du jus de cuisson. Faites cuire jusqu'à ce que le jus épaississe puis ajoutez 50 ml de crème et 20 g de beurre. Mélangez doucement l'ensemble jusqu'à ce que la crème et le beurre forment une émulsion homogène. Dans une poêle chaude, faites chauffer un peu d'huile d'olive. Assaisonnez les langoustines puis faites les cuire pendant 1 minute en les retournant une fois. Mettez un peu des haricots sur chaque assiette, placez une langoustine dessus avec les pousses de pois et les lambeaux de jambon. Versez de la sauce aux haricots tout autour.

300 g de alubias frescas
1 zanahoria, pelada y partida por la mitad
1 cebolla pelada partida en cuartos
2 chalotes grandes, pelados y partidos en cuartos
150 g de beicon ahumado
100 ml de nata
50 g de cebolla cortada en cubitos
40 g de mantequilla
1 ramita de tomillo
25 g de jamón de Jabugo en cubitos
4 cigalas crudas grandes peladas
2 tajadas de jamón de Jabugo
Guisantes aliñados con un poco de vinagreta
Aceite de oliva
Sal y pimienta

Lleve las alubias a ebullición, escúrralas y enjuáguelas con agua fría. Póngalas de nuevo en la olla con la zanahoria, la cebolla, los chalotes y el beicon. Cúbralas con agua fría y cuézalas durante 30 minutos, hasta que estén tiernas. Sáquelas y reserve el agua de cocción. Tome la mitad de las alubias y la mitad del líquido de cocción y lleve a ebullición junto con la mitad (50 ml) de la nata. Condimente con sal y pimienta. Manténgalas calientes y bátalas suavemente antes de servir. Cueza la cebolla junto con el tomillo en 20 g de mantequilla a fuego lento, hasta que esté cocida pero no dorada. Retire el tomillo y reserve. Selle el jamón de Jabugo en una sartén con poco aceite de oliva y añada la cebolla cocida, las alubias restantes y 50 ml del líquido de cocción. Cueza hasta que espese y agregue los 50 ml de nata restantes y 20 g de mantequilla. Remueva bien hasta que la nata y la mantequilla se mezclen completamente. En una sartén caliente un poco de aceite de oliva. Salpimiente las cigalas y cuézalas durante un minuto y luego déles la vuelta. Sirva una porción de alubias en cada plato, coloque las cigalas encima junto con los guisantes y las tiras de jamón de Jabugo. Rocíe la salsa de alubias alrededor.

Ubon

Design: United Designers | Executive Chef: Nobuyuki Matsuhisa
Head Chef London: Mark Edwards

34 West Ferry Circus, Canary Wharf | Docklands, E14 8RR
Phone: +44 20 7719 7800
www.noburestaurants.com
Tube: Canary Wharf
Opening hours: Lunch Mo–Fri 12 noon to 2:30 pm, dinner Mo–Sat 6.00 pm to
10.15 pm
Average price: £50
Cuisine: Modern Japanese

Lobster Salad

with spicy lemon dressing

Hummersalat mit würzigem Zitronendressing
Salade de homard avec une sauce épicée au citron
Ensalada de bogavante con aderezo picante de limón

1 lb 5 oz live lobster (boil for 5 minutes, then plunge into icy water)
2 handfuls of mixed salad greens
One third of a cucumber thinly sliced
4 shitake mushrooms (cooked in a hot pan)
Freshly snipped chives
A good pinch of toasted white sesame seeds

Spicy lemon dressing:
50 ml of grapeseed oil
Juice of half a lemon
A tsp of Soy sauce
A pinch of salt
A pinch of Cayenne pepper
A pinch of cracked black pepper
A glove of garlic, crushed

Combine all the ingredients for the dressing except the oil. When the salt is fully dissolved, add oil.
Remove meat from lobster.
Toss the leaves and cucumber in some of the dressing.
Arrange the leaves and cucumber on a plate.
Lean the lobster meat against the salad.
Garnish with shitake mushrooms, a sprinkling of Sesame seeds and chives.
Finish by drizzling some of the remaining dressing around the plate and on top of the lobster.

650 g lebender Hummer (5 Minuten kochen, dann in Eiswasser tauchen)
2 handvoll gemischter Salatblätter
Ein Drittel Gurke, in dünne Scheiben geschnitten
4 Shitake Pilze (in der heißen Pfanne gebraten)
Schnittlauch, frisch geschnitten
Eine große Prise weißer Sesamkerne, geröstet

Würziges Zitronendressing:
50 ml Traubenkernöl
Saft einer halben Zitrone
1 TL Sojasoße
1 Prise Salz
1 Prise Cayennepfeffer
1 Prise schwarzen Pfeffer, gemahlen
1 Knoblauchzehe, gepresst

Alle Zutaten, bis auf das Öl, vermischen und es erst dann hinzufügen, wenn sich das Salz vollkommen aufgelöst hat.
Das Fleisch vom Hummer lösen.
Salatblätter und Gurke mit etwas Dressing anmachen und sie dann auf einem Teller platzieren.
Legen Sie das Hummerfleisch neben den Salat. Garnieren Sie mit Shitake Pilzen und streuen Sie Sesam und Schnittlauch darüber.
Zum Schluss geben Sie noch etwas Dressing über den Hummer und verzieren Sie den Tellerrand mit dem restlichen Dressing.

1 homard vivant de 650 g (faites-le bouillir
5 minutes puis plongez-le dans de l'eau
garnie de glaçons)
2 poignées de feuilles de différentes salades
Le tiers d'un concombre coupé en fines
tranches
4 champignons shitake (cuits dans une
casserole très chaude)
De la ciboulette fraîchement cueillie
Une bonne pincée de graines de sésame
blanches grillées

Sauce épicée au citron :
50 ml d'huile de graines de raisin
Le jus d'un demi-citron
Une c. à café de sauce au soja
Une pincée de sel
Une pincée de poivre de Cayenne
Une pincée de poivre noir mouliné
Une gousse d'ail écrasée

Réunissez tous les ingrédients de la sauce,
sauf l'huile. N'ajoutez l'huile qu'une fois le
sel entièrement dissous.
Détachez la chair du homard.
Déposez les feuilles de salade et les tranches fines du concombre dans un peu de la
sauce.
Disposez les feuilles et le concombre sur
un plat.
Déposez la chair du homard sur les feuilles
de salade. Garnissez avec les champignons
shitake, saupoudrez les graines de sésame
et la ciboulette.
Finissez en versant tout doucement la
sauce restante autour du plat et sur la
chair de homard.

650 g de bogavante, vivo (cocer 5 minutos, luego meter en agua helada)
2 puñados de hojas de ensaladas variadas
Un tercio de pepino, cortado en rodajas
finas
4 hongos Shiitake (fritos en la sartén a
fuego fuerte)
Cebollino, recién cortado
Una pizca grande de semillas tostadas de
sésamo blanco

Aderezo picante de limón:
50 ml aceite de pepitas de uva
El zumo de medio limón
1 cucharadita de salsa de soja
1 pizca de sal
1 pizca de pimienta de cayena
1 pizca de pimienta negra molida
1 diente de ajo, machacado

Mezclar todos los ingredientes, excepto el
aceite, y agregar este último cuando se
haya disuelto completamente la sal.
Desprender la carne del bogavante.
Aderezar las hojas de ensalada y el pepino
con una pequeña cantidad de aderezo y
colocar sobre un plato.
Colocar el bogavante junto a la ensalada.
Guarnecer con los hongos shiitake y espar-
cir las semillas de sésamo y el cebollino
por encima.
Finalmente, añada otra pequeña cantidad
de aderezo sobre el bogavante y decore el
borde del plato con el resto del aderezo.

Zuma

Design: Noriyoshi Muramatsu for Super Potato, Tokyo

5 Raphael Street | Knightsbridge, SW7 NC11
Phone: +44 20 7584 1010
www.zumarestaurant.com | info@zumarestaurant.com
Tube: Knightsbridge
Opening hours: Lunch Mon–Sat 12 noon to 2:30 pm, dinner 6 pm to 11:30 pm,
Sun 12 noon to 3 pm & 6 pm to 10:30 pm
Price range: Lunch £15, dinner £40
Cuisine: Japanese